AF614031

Foreword

There are many things that can be said about the author of this book. Barbara has such a humble spirit coupled with a quiet but strong demeanor while encompassing a Christ-like love for people. These are just some of the great characteristics that help define Barbara, however, make no mistake about it, her God-given ability to overcome her circumstances, her faith in God to see a brighter future, and by her unquenchable desire to fulfill God's plan for her life, has given her the platform to speak such needed understanding about one of the greatest stories ever told by Jesus.

If you ever felt like you were meant for more, yet have settled for less in life, this book, "The Woman at the Well" is for you. Its proven biblical insights will bring hope to your life and inspire you to rise to a greater place. Barbara's powerful yet vulnerable teaching grabbed my heart and stirred my soul to believe that there is hope for those who have had to overcome insurmountable odds. With this book, Barbara builds upon the inspiring message from the woman at the well that will help real people in the real world to break through whatever barriers they have encountered.

I agree with Barbara, "The Lord Jesus doesn't give us life-changing experiences to keep them to ourselves". This story serves as a model for that truth and instills hope for many who have a desire for more in life. I know as you read this book, you will not only be encouraged but also challenged to be the best person you were created to be.

The Woman at the Well

The Woman at the Well

A Story of Redemption

By Barbara Kelly

Copyright © 2013 Barbara Kelly.

All rights reserved. No part of this book may be used or reproduced by any means, graphic, electronic, or mechanical, including photocopying, recording, taping or by any information storage retrieval system without the written permission of the publisher except in the case of brief quotations embodied in critical articles and reviews.

WestBow Press books may be ordered through booksellers or by contacting:

WestBow Press
A Division of Thomas Nelson
1663 Liberty Drive
Bloomington, IN 47403
www.westbowpress.com
1-(866) 928-1240

Because of the dynamic nature of the Internet, any web addresses or links contained in this book may have changed since publication and may no longer be valid. The views expressed in this work are solely those of the author and do not necessarily reflect the views of the publisher, and the publisher hereby disclaims any responsibility for them.

Any people depicted in stock imagery provided by Thinkstock are models, and such images are being used for illustrative purposes only.
Certain stock imagery © Thinkstock.

Scriptures taken from the Holy Bible, New International Version®, NIV®. Copyright © 1973, 1978, 1984, 2011 by Biblica, Inc.™ Used by permission of Zondervan. All rights reserved worldwide. www.zondervan.com The "NIV" and "New International Version" are trademarks registered in the United States Patent and Trademark Office by Biblica, Inc.™ All rights reserved.

ISBN: 978-1-4497-8331-0 (sc)
ISBN: 978-1-4497-8332-7 (hc)
ISBN: 978-1-4497-8330-3 (e)
Library of Congress Control Number: 2013903688

Printed in the United States of America

WestBow Press rev. date: 3/7/2013

Acknowledgments

To my children, Jessica and Jason, who have weathered this journey with me, not without suffering their own hurts and triumphantly serving Christ with their whole heart. I love you.

To Pastor Jimmy Myers, Christian Life Center, Fallon, NV for teaching the Word and always being there for my family.

To Pastors Leonard and Jeanne Arlint, River of Life Faith Church, Fallon, NV, for being my dear friends for the past 30 years and giving me solid Biblical advice when I needed it and for praying for and loving us unconditionally.

To Pastor Leo Kruger, Valley Christian Fellowship, Gardnerville, NV for showing me the genuine love of Christ when I was at my darkest hour.

To Pastors Chris and DeDe Vigil, Victory City Church, Sparks, NV for teaching us God's Grace and the Glory and the Power of God.

Contents

1 The Woman at the Well 1

2 Shattered Dreams.. 7

3 Shame.. 17

4 Fear 27

5 Unequally Yoked 35

6 Adultery 45

7 Counseling 51

8 Who Are We? 57

9 Stand up and Take your rightful place 63

10 Prayer 69

11 Praise and Worship 75

12 Glory!..81

Conclusion Now Go Forth! 87

PREFACE

But the fruit of the Spirit is love, joy, peace, patience, kindness, goodness, gentleness and self-control. (Galatians 5:22&23) NIV

LOVE, JOY, PEACE, PATIENCE, KINDNESS, GOODNESS, GENTLENESS and self-control, these are such things that I lived by day by day for the last thirty some years serving our Lord, so how did I come to this place that I am right now. Four failed marriages. How on earth does a born-again, spirit-filled woman get to this point in her life. Broken hearted, hurt, angry, disappointed, ready to give up on everything, how does this happen? This journey that I am on with the Lord has been a long hard road but I would not change one single life lesson I have learned. The woman at the well sounds just like me. I can relate to her story but it is not a story of shame and judgment, but a story of our Lord's grace, mercy and forgiveness. Over the course of this book we are going to explore "the amazing grace that saved a wretch like me" and the wonderful revelations that I have come to understand through my personal relationship with the Lord.

Before we get started, I have to make it clear that this is a story of restoration and hope for someone who was hopeless. On Easter Sunday 1980 the most wonderful life changing event happened in my life that would spin my life into a different direction, a direction with purpose and healing of past hurts. I was in a church, a dry old church, filled with singing stale hymns, gossiping and having Sunday pot lucks. I needed something in my life and that was the only place I knew to go. The Lord met me where I was at, a predestined, pre-appointed time in my life during that particular Sunday service. The Lord will meet you where you are.

You see, my parents had come from backgrounds of bad church experiences and did not really understand the meaning of salvation. My father had been raised Catholic and ran away from home when he was seventeen enlisting in the Navy. He hated his strict upbringing and did not want me to be exposed to the Catholic religion. I have often wondered because of the stories he had told me about his childhood if he had been one of victims of child molestation that has been come to be known as very prevalent in the Catholic Church. He was a man of few words and in the 70 years of adulthood he only returned home to see his family twice.

My mother on the other hand had been raised in a different church, The Reorganized Church of Latter Day Saints and she had told me stories of the minister yelling at the congregation about going to hell and she would leave service with a pounding headache. So she was not inclined to go to church either. So there I was, always knowing there was something more, something missing, just couldn't put my finger on it and then that Easter Sunday 1980 I found myself in church hearing the story of Jesus dying on the cross and rising again. There was no altar call but the Lord met me right where I was and my heart was ready to receive Him. I knew I needed something and there He was. His love flowed over me with such a powerful calm and for the first time in my life I understood what love was. The weight of the world was physically lifted off of me and I began to weep until I had no more tears left.

I want to take a brief moment before we continue to give you the opportunity to receive Jesus as your Savior and allow Him to heal the hurts you might be carrying. You can pray this prayer.

"Heavenly Father, I surrender, I ask for Your forgiveness of my sins, I have lived my life according to my rules and I keep getting stuck in the same patterns, Please Lord forgive me and help me to get my life back on track to where You would have me be."

In Jesus Precious Name I pray. Amen.

If you prayed that prayer for the first time I encourage you to contact a church that believes the Bible is the living Word of God and attend so you can learn what the Bible says and also get to know other Believers to help you with this new journey you are about to embark on.

Every person's life, no matter how they were raised or what traumatic things have happened, has one thing in common. Everyone was created by God for a purpose, and He can heal and use what was meant for evil and turn it around to use for good in our lives. The story in the Bible, in the book of John, the fourth chapter, talks about a wonderful story of the woman at the well. This is story showing that someone at their worst can be forgiven, and the Lord is full of mercy and grace.

CHAPTER 1

THE WOMAN AT THE WELL

The woman said, "I know that Messiah" (called Christ) "is coming. When he comes, he will explain everything to us." Then Jesus declared, "I, the one speaking to you—I am he." John 4:25-26 NIV

ONCE UPON A TIME THERE WAS A woman, a woman that would be nameless. She had suffered much in her life and had been the ridicule of the community. She had no idea that day as she went to get water from the well that she was about to experience a miracle, a predestined meeting with the Lord Jesus Christ and her life as well as the lives of many others were about to be changed forever. How many of us are wounded and need this type of encounter with the Lord for a life changing experience?

This story is a powerful reminder of God's grace. The Lord saw through all of the pain and the shame and hard life that this woman had lived. He was sitting at the well waiting as she approached and He startled her by starting a conversation with her. As they spoke He divulged details of her life to her and she was shocked He knew so much about her. Can you imagine a complete stranger coming up to you and speaking out-loud the events of your personal life? He knew every secret and He began to speak of them as fact without condemnation.

During the course of this story we will look at this scripture and we will share the Revelation of the Lord and His wonderful power, mercy and forgiveness that He has shown me that you too can have in your life.

The Woman at the Well

John 4:4 Now he (Jesus) had to go through Samaria. 5 So he came to a town in Samaria called Sychar, near the plot of ground Jacob had given to his son Joseph. 6 Jacob's well was there, and Jesus, tired as he was from the journey, sat down by the well. It was about noon.

7 When a Samaritan woman came to draw water, Jesus said to her, "Will you give me a drink?" 8 (His disciples had gone into the town to buy food.)

9 The Samaritan woman said to him, "You are a Jew and I am a Samaritan woman. How can you ask me for a drink?" (For Jews do not associate with Samaritans.)

In Hebrew the name Samaria is Shomron , meaning literally watch tower. The town was located in the heart of the mountains of Judea or commonly known as Israel. It had been besieged by several different Kings who in turn deported undesirables from their own territories to live in Samaria. It was a town with many different mixed races and peoples. It is believed John the Baptists' body is buried there.

2 Kings 6:24[Famine in Besieged Samaria] Some time later, Ben-Hadad king of Aram mobilized his entire army and marched up and laid siege to Samaria.

2 Kings 17:5 The king of Assyria invaded the entire land, marched against Samaria and laid siege to it for three years.

In Jesus lifetime there was a definite demarcation between the Jewish people and the Samaritans. The Jews were not to talk to or have anything to do with them.

Matthew 10:5 These twelve Jesus sent out with the following instructions: "Do not go among the Gentiles or enter any town of the Samaritans.

Jesus crossed the lines between cultures showing His Grace and Love to this woman giving her life.

John 4:10 Jesus answered her, "If you knew the gift of God and who it is that asks you for a drink, you would have asked him and he would have given you living water.'

11 "Sir," the woman said, "you have nothing to draw with and the well is deep. Where can you get this living water? 12 Are you greater than our father Jacob, who gave us the well and drank from it himself, as did also his sons and his livestock?"

13 Jesus answered, "Everyone who drinks this water will be thirsty again, 14 but whoever drinks the water I give them will never thirst. Indeed, the water I give them will become in them a spring of water welling up to eternal life."

15 The woman said to him, "Sir, give me this water so that I won't get thirsty and have to keep coming here to draw water."

16 He told her, "Go, call your husband and come back."

17 "I have no husband," she replied. Jesus said to her, "You are right when you say you have no husband. 18 The fact is, you have had five husbands, and the man you now have is not your husband. What you have just said is quite true."

Jesus had a word of knowledge about the woman. When He told her details of her personal life, she knew then there was something different about Him and questioned if He was a prophet.

One of the gifts of the Holy Spirit that are active today is the word of knowledge. This gift of the word of knowledge is a supernatural revelation of the divine will and plan of God from God.

1 Corinthians 12: 7 Now to each one the manifestation of the Spirit is given for the common good. 8 To one there is given through the Spirit a message of wisdom, to another a message of knowledge by means of the same Spirit, 9 to another faith by the same Spirit, to another gifts of healing by that one Spirit, 10 to another miraculous powers, to another prophecy, to another distinguishing between spirits, to another speaking in different kinds of tongues,[a] and to still another the interpretation of tongues.[b] 11 All these are the work of one and the same Spirit, and he distributes them to each one, just as he determines.

John 4:19 "Sir," the woman said, "I can see that you are a prophet. 20 Our ancestors worshiped on this mountain, but you Jews claim that the place where we must worship is in Jerusalem."

21 "Woman," Jesus replied, "believe me, a time is coming when you will worship the Father neither on this mountain nor in Jerusalem.

22 You Samaritans worship what you do not know; we worship what we do know, for salvation is from the Jews. 23 Yet a time is coming and has now come when the true worshipers will worship the Father in the Spirit and in truth, for they are the kind of worshipers the Father seeks. 24 God is spirit, and his worshipers must worship in the Spirit and in truth."

25 The woman said, "I know that Messiah" (called Christ) "is coming. When he comes, he will explain everything to us."

26 Then Jesus declared, "I, the one speaking to you—I am he." NIV

What a wonderful experience for the woman. Jesus himself, offering her Living Water that she would never be thirsty again. These are the promises that we can have in our lives if we come to the well to drink and drink of the Living Water.

Although Jesus had words of knowledge of the woman's life, He did not condemn her, He only brought up the subject to give credence that He was the Messiah and knew all things. He had the power of the Father and the Holy Spirit and could offer forgiveness and unconditional acceptance in a way that this woman had never known before.

John 4:27-30 Just then his disciples returned and were surprised to find him talking with a woman. But no one asked, "What do you want?" or "Why are you talking with her?" Then, leaving her water jar, the woman went back to the town and said to the people, 29 "Come, see a man who told me everything I ever did. Could this be the Messiah?" 30 They came out of the town and made their way toward him.

John 4:39 Many of the Samaritans from that town believed in him because of the woman's testimony, "He told me everything I ever did."

The Lord Jesus doesn't give us life changing experiences to keep them to ourselves. His miracles and his unconditional love are to be spread to other people's lives so they can have their own encounter with Him and understand He is the Son of God.

John 4:40-42 So when the Samaritans came to him, they urged him to stay with them, and he stayed two days. And because of his words many more became believers. They said to the woman, "We no longer believe just because of what you said; now we have heard for ourselves, and we know that this man really is the Savior of the world."

Chapter 2

Shattered Dreams

The man said, "This is now bone of my bones and flesh of my flesh; she shall be called 'woman,' for she was taken out of man." That is why a man leaves his father and mother and is united to his wife, and they become one flesh.

(Genesis 2:23-24)NIV

Grace Kelly: I love Grace Kelly. Growing up in the "60's" I was enamored with her beauty and grace. She was so elegant and proper and so admired as a lady. I couldn't help but to want to be like her. Born in 1929 she became a famous actress living the fairy tale life of marrying the Prince Rainier III of Monaco. She had the perfect parents, her dad was an Olympic gold medal winner and self-made millionaire, her mother was the first coach of women's athletic teams at the University of Pennsylvania. Grace was an accomplished actress performing in the movies "Rear Window", "Dial M for Murder" and "To Catch a Thief". Isn't this the dream of every little girl to be beautiful, admired and marry a Prince?

Dreams quickly became shattered with a life of victimization causing my life to go in directions I had never planned on it to go. In writing this book I started out with the idea of analyzing the whys and wherefores of why I have been a victim and along the journey I came to the place of healing through the love of my Lord, Jesus Christ. I am a Child of the King, Daughter of the Most High God and nothing can detour me from the assignment the Lord has given me to fulfill. Praise the Lord for His Grace, Mercy, Forgiveness and Unconditional Love! If God is for us who can be against us? Right?

Romans 8:30-39 And those he predestined, he also called; those he called, he also justified; those he justified, he also glorified.

31 What, then, shall we say in response to these things? If God is for us, who can be against us?

32 He who did not spare his own Son, but gave him up for us all—how will he not also, along with him, graciously give us all things?

33 Who will bring any charge against those whom God has chosen? It is God who justifies.

34Who then is the one who condemns? No one. Christ Jesus who died—more than that, who was raised to life—is at the right hand of God and is also interceding for us.

35 Who shall separate us from the love of Christ? Shall trouble or hardship or persecution or famine or nakedness or danger or sword?

36 As it is written: "For your sake we face death all day long; we are considered as sheep to be slaughtered."

37 No, in all these things we are more than conquerors through him who loved us.

38 For I am convinced that neither death nor life, neither angels nor demons, neither the present nor the future, nor any powers,

39 neither height nor depth, nor anything else in all creation, will be able to separate us from the love of God that is in Christ Jesus our Lord. raised to life—is at the right hand of God and is also interceding for us.

So how does so much tragedy happen in one person's life? We all ask the question of why in our lives. This is an age old question that everyone asked about varying degrees of tragedies in their lives. I don't believe we will ever know the whole truth about our particular circumstances until we are sitting at the feet of Jesus, but I do know that from the moment of conception we were made for a Godly purpose here on earth and the enemy will do every possible thing to stop of from fulfilling our calling.

Psalms 139:13-14 For you created my inmost being; you knit me together in my mother's womb. I praise you because I am fearfully and wonderfully made; your works are wonderful, I know that full well.

I believe in Heaven and I also believe in hell, and the fallen angels have been on assignment from the day of Satan's fall to destroy God's chosen people.

I Peter 5:8 Be self-controlled and alert. Your enemy the devil prowls around like a roaring lion looking for someone to devour.

The higher your calling the harder the enemy pursues you. Do we need to be afraid? Never! Fear is one of the enemy's tools that he uses against us.

Isaiah 41:10 So do not fear, for I am with you; do not be dismayed, for I am your God.

I will strengthen you and help you; I will uphold you with my righteous right hand.

So instead of focusing on the whys', move on to the how can I get over this? C.S. Lewis said once, "Can a mortal ask questions which God finds unanswerable? Quite easily, I should think. All nonsense questions are unanswerable." So stop dwelling on the things of the past that you might never quite understand and start declaring to the Heavens what should be for your future.

2 Corinthians 10:4-6 4 The weapons we fight with are not the weapons of the world. On the contrary, they have divine power to demolish strongholds. 5 We demolish arguments and every pretension that sets itself up against the knowledge of God, and we take captive every thought to make it obedient to Christ. 6 And we will be ready to punish every act of disobedience, once your obedience is complete.

We need to bring our very thought process, cleansed with the power of the Holy Spirit to conform with the Word of God and with the Mind of Christ. We ALL are chosen to be perfected by His Spirit and move forward.

1 Corinthians 2:15-16 The person with the Spirit makes judgments about all things, but such a person is not subject to merely human judgments, for, "Who has known the mind of the Lord so as to instruct him?" But we have the mind of Christ.

The Samaritan woman was able to start the healing process of not being fearful. As she spoke to the Lord she began to recognize who He was.

John10 Jesus answered her, "If you knew the gift of God and who it is that asks you for a drink, you would have asked him and he would have given you living water."

11 "Sir," the woman said, "you have nothing to draw with and the well is deep. Where can you get this living water? 12 Are you greater than our father Jacob, who gave us the well and drank from it himself, as did also his sons and his livestock?"

Is it that easy? No, not in the practical everyday hectic lives we live but we must overcome and move into a place where our relationship with the Lord is number one in our lives and nothing else matters. I remember being fearful most of my life of everything, always waiting for the next trauma to come. My children went up in a small prop plane for a ride with a pilot friend of ours and I was fearful and didn't go. We lived in a rural area and the plane flew close over my house as I was outside watching. The enemy came in and filled my head with fear and thoughts of what would happen if they crashed and I lost them all. I began to pray out of my fear for the Lord to protect my family and the Lord spoke to me very clearly and said, "What if I chose to take them this day would you still serve Me?" That was a hard question to answer but yes wholeheartedly yes, I can't imagine my life any other way. I told the Lord of course I would serve Him until the day I die. We have to be able to change our minds and not give into the fears and the emotions that cause us to stumble. That means every day you have to bathe your mind with praise and worship of our most High God and allow Him to direct your life. We have been created to worship Him and every day and every hour and every minute has an appointed assignment in the Heavens. So before allowing those thoughts of anger and fear to come upon you, begin singing and praising the Lord. I believe we are in a new season of God's grace like we have never seen before. People all over the world are coming together in masses to sing, dance and praise the Lord. Strongholds will be broken and souls will be saved. When we praise the Lord, all of Heaven praises with us, breaking into singing and dancing and playing beautiful music. We must break out of our old routines and praise the Lord. There is a supernatural movement all over the world going on where God's glory is touching earth and many miracles and healing are taking place because God's people are praising and worshiping Him. So today, worship the Lord with all you have in you. Sing, dance, and shout and praise the Lord with all you have and watch and see the break through that happens in your life! I dare you!

Deuteronomy 26:18-19 NIV And the Lord has declared this day that you are his people, his treasured possession as he promised, and that you are to keep all his commands. He has declared that he will set you in praise, fame and honor high above all the nations he has made and that you will be a people holy to the Lord your God, as he promised.

So why does tragedy happen?

Matthew 5:44-45 (NIV) But I tell you, love your enemies and pray for those who persecute you, that you may be children of your Father in heaven. He causes his sun to rise on the evil and the good, and sends rain on the righteous and the unrighteous.

Sin goes back to the day Eve ate the apple. Good versus evil. The statistics are staggering and you are not alone in your situation.

Many women are attacked by the enemy early in their lives by physical, emotional and sexual abuse in order to thwart their ability to fulfill their calling and their destiny in Christ. The enemy had come against me in this way when I was only five years old. I was sexually molested at that tender age. At that age a mere baby does not know how to say no or fight back or even tell. No one in my family had known it happened or at least never let on that it had happened. This type of abuse shakes a child to their very core of whom they are in Christ, stealing away their belief in who they are and what their purpose is, causing a domino effect with every relationship after the victimization. I never told anyone and had buried it in the back of mind. I did not have a recollection of the details of the incident but it caused significant damage in the way I perceived relationships. When I was thirty years old the person who had molested me had died. I was devastated and I cried out to God and was angry. I looked up to him and loved him so much but had not dealt with the memories of the abuse and it was always nagging at my unconscious mind. The underlying emotion of betrayal constantly was with me. I was angry at the Lord that this person had not reconciled himself, knowing Christ as his Savior and had not been forgiven and had been doomed to hell forever. As I cried out to the Lord, He spoke to me and said, "You don't know everything, just because you didn't lead him to Me personally doesn't mean I didn't meet him where he was in My perfect timing. If I rescued you, do you not think I would rescue him?" I had to repent of my narrow mindedness. The Lord asked me if I wanted to remember the details of the abuse and I asked Him if it was important for me to remember and He said no, I just needed to remember that He is my Creator with the ability to turn every situation around and heal me." I chose not to revisit the details and today I am completely healed of the situation.

Although a sad situation, many people continue to be the victim because it is familiar to them and sometimes being healed and the unknown are much more terrifying than living in the belief they are a victim. Many victims become perpetrators and enablers of others in much the same way they were victimized.

According to the U. S. Justice Department statistics roughly 33% of girls and 14% of boys are molested before the age of 18. And they also state they believe that only 35% of sexual abuse of minors is reported. So the odds are you have been a victim or someone close to you has been a victim. Sexual sins have been occurring since the beginning of time.

Genesis 34:2 (NIV) When Shechem son of Hamor the Hivite, the ruler of that area, saw her, he took her and raped her.

It is no less damaging today as it was back then; the only difference today is our society has been flooded with so much emphasis on sexual exploits that it causes us to be desensitized to the fact that it does devastating emotional damage to all who are abused in this way. According the FBI crime statistics for the year 2011 there were an estimated 83,425 forcible rapes reported to law enforcement.

Domestic violence is another of the enemy's attacks. If he can cause division in the family core he can manipulate many lives and many generations off of their course that the Lord has ordained in their lives. The statistics are staggering but with the Lord we have hope to overcome these things in our past and use them for good. With so many victims, the odds that we can use our story to help many have a revelation of god; healing power can be a driving force and focus for us to move on and allow the Lord to heal us. Surrendering and allow the Lord to heal us is so much easier than hiding from those things that haunt us.

Prayer

Heavenly Father,You are our Jehovah Rapha (Healer). Nothing that comes against us stands between Your Love and ourselves. Please show us the areas that we need healing and are vulnerable in and send Your waves of peace and healing to fill those areas. In Jesus Precious Name

Reflection

Ask yourself where do I need healing?

Do I have unforgiveness for others or myself?

What are the dreams that I have given up?

Chapter 3

Shame

If I am guilty—woe to me! Even if I am innocent, I cannot lift my head, for I am full of shame and drowned in my affliction. Job 10:15 NIV

Ten times now you have reproached me;
shamelessly you attack me. Job 19:3NIV

Shame on you! You should be ashamed of yourself! Have you no shame? These are words we have heard when we have done something that might not have been quite acceptable to people around us. The woman at the well felt shame over her failed marriages and public humiliation. She would go to get water for her family during the middle of day to avoid meeting up with the other women who would go either in the morning or the evening to gather their water and they would go in groups for safety and fellowship. She was an outcast. We have all felt ashamed at some point in our life and have avoided people in our lives because we did not want to be humiliated. What does shame actually mean?

Definition of shame according to the American Heritage dictionary:

**A painful emotion caused by a strong sense of guilt, embarrassment, unworthiness, or disgrace.

★★One that brings dishonor, disgrace, or condemnation.

★★A condition of disgrace or dishonor; ignominy.

★★A great disappointment.

John 4:5-6 NIV So he (Jesus) came to a town in Samaria called Sychar, near the plot of ground Jacob had given to his son Joseph. Jacob's well was there, and Jesus, tired as he was from the journey, sat down by the well. It was about noon.

Can you imagine the shame that this woman had felt? I can. Every failed marriage caused deeper emotional damage and whittled away at my feeling of self-worth. Shame is not the same as guilt. If we have repented of the things we have done, we are forgiven. It's as simple as that, but the enemy comes in and pressures our senses with thoughts of shame including sending people to remind us of our inequities, causing more damage. He bombards us with circumstances in order to beat us down and cause us to hide from the people that can love us and help us heal through these situations. The story of Job is a perfect example. He did nothing wrong and the Lord allowed the enemy to come against him to test his faithfulness to the Lord.

Job 10:15 NIV If I am guilty—woe to me! Even if I am innocent, I cannot lift my head, for I am full of shame and drowned in my affliction.

When I began to write this book I had to think back on the shameful moments of my life. In a nutshell, my first marriage I was married at 18 years old had a child at 19 years and the married dissolved when I was 20 years old. I did not know the Lord and this was the most difficult marriage because at such a tender age I just wanted to be married and live happily ever after. My husband and his family were atheists and now as I look back, the Lord took me out of the situation because He knew the plans He had for me.

Jeremiah 29:11(NIV) For I know the plans I have for you," declares the

Lord, "plans to prosper you and not to harm you, plans to give you hope and a future.

I didn't understand the calling of the Lord on my life and I was so full of shame and felt like such a failure. This was the beginning time of trying to find what was missing in my life and led me to the foot of the cross of Jesus. Although each marriage failing was devastating I am not blaming anyone but myself. I have been healed and each person is in varying states of their relationship with the Lord. I could analyze the situations and expose details but it would cause harm and not good, and that is not the intention of this book. This is the story of my life and my healing and the possibility of healing of hurting women all over that are facing similar situations in their lives.

My first marriage was one without Christ. Needless to say it's hard enough with the Lord to keep marriages intact but without Him it's almost impossible. I really hadn't had a positive example of what a good marriage should be.

The birth of my first child made me start thinking about the spiritual side of life and I was drawn to the Lord and knew there was something I was missing in my life.

My second marriage was ten years long and during this time I had my second child. This marriage was a Christian marriage but there were so many spiritual things that were awry. We were babies in Christ and did not know how to use the power of the Holy Spirit to overcome. This marriage was filled with violence and I had no choice but to leave for my safety and my children's safety. My spouse was a victim of Post-traumatic Stress Disorder from being in Viet Nam. There was such an overwhelming spiritual attack on the veterans that were over there. And unfortunately many are still dealing with the devastation.

My third and fourth marriages were ones of rebounding and not seeking the Lord's will in my life. I was weak and feelings of unworthiness caused me to be blind to the signs that were right in front of me that this was not where the Lord wanted me to be. We were unequally yoked in both situations which lead to agony in not being able to fulfill the calling on my life. Our beliefs were so different that there was no way I was going to thrive and be the woman God has called me to be and to please them. I placed myself in situations not ordained for my life by God and without the covering of the Lord. It was very hard to keep my head above water spiritually let alone be productive and produce fruit for my Lord Jesus.

I have always had an underlying low self-esteem causing me to not stand up for myself. When I meet people in particular I overlook the "red flags" or signs from the Lord that I need to flee. Do you think the Samaritan woman felt the same way? She wanted someone to take care of her as was the culture back then. Without a provider and a protector she would be vulnerable to both verbal and physical attacks. Who knows what her childhood had been like? Did her father give her in marriage the first time at a tender age as was the culture? Did he father give her to a man who was abusive? Was she a virgin as the culture at the time had called every woman given in marriage to be? Had she been sexually molested or raped as a child? Had she been a victim of physical abuse as she grew up? Who were these men she had been married to and why did they divorce her? Did they have affairs and divorce her for someone else? Did they divorce her because she had been unfaithful? All these questions come to mind because we don't know the circumstances of her life and how she ended up at the well at that moment. But the important thing to remember is Jesus was there at exactly the right moment in time and gave her the gift of life and living water.

She no doubt had been full of shame. Shame is a recurring theme all through the Bible. There are scriptures where the Lord condemns people and allows them to feel their shame in order for them to turn from the ways that are separating them from the love of God but there are also many scriptures that show that we don't have to be punished by our shame because He is a God of mercy and grace.

Isaiah 43:18-19 (KJV)"Remember ye not the former things, neither consider the things of old. Behold, I will do a new thing; now it shall spring forth; shall ye not know it? I will even make a way in the wilderness, and rivers in the desert." Isaiah 61:7 (NIV) "Instead of your shame you will receive a double portion, and instead of disgrace you will rejoice in your inheritance. And so you will inherit a double portion in your land, and everlasting joy will be yours. Proverbs 13:18 (KJV) "Poverty and shame shall be to him that refuseth instruction: but he that regardeth reproof shall be honoured."

Isaiah 54:4 (KJV) "Fear not; for thou shalt not be ashamed: neither be thou confounded; for thou shalt not be put to shame: for thou shalt forget the shame of thy youth, and shalt not remember the reproach of thy widowhood anymore."

We can be overcomers and not feel the shame of our weaknesses and we can be completely healed by the power of the Holy Spirit.

There are different ways shame can come upon us. The enemy can place thoughts that we dwell on to belittling ourselves or chastise ourselves. Another way is through people who don't have our best interest at heart can come against us with accusing words trying to knock us down. How do we deal with these things? The first thing is immersing ourselves in the Word, letting His promises wash over us constantly. The Word is alive and it brings healing and if we live in the Word it will live in us. So whenever those thoughts of negativity come against us, we must tell them to go. We are children of the Lord and the Word says heirs to the throne so it does not matter what we or other people think. We know who we are.

People who want to do us harm are a little harder to deal with. Trying to keep our confidence up when someone is beating us down with their condemning words or actions can be a challenge. Praying for our enemies, (yes even those who love us can be our enemies) is crucial and being nonjudgmental toward them. Let the love that God has for them permeate your prayer life. Praise, worship and declare blessings over their lives. When they attack you, tell them "bless you!" You will see a turnaround; the Word cannot go out void. Speak peace and confidence over their lives. Declare that what is in Heaven will touch Earth and manifest in their lives. Speak life not death! You may not see the difference in the physical realm but there will be a shift in the spiritual realm and eventually will show in the natural. Declare restoration in your family. Declare a break through and breaking of generational curses and then praise God for the changes even before you see them manifest.

Isaiah 51:7NIV"Hear me, you who know what is right, you people who have taken my instruction to heart: Do not fear the reproach of mere mortals or be terrified by their insults.

Sometimes even people that are close to us can cause us grief in this area. Why would someone who loves us want you to feel ashamed? When we are restored and healed the people around us see the transformation in us and it makes them uncomfortable. It causes them to have to look at their own shame and it is easier to try and bring us back to the former place of defeat because it is familiar ground for them. They know how to act in familiar situations and don't have to examine their own lives and failures. Being set free is unknown territory. It makes those around us uncomfortable, they don't know how to act or react.

Isaiah 35:4 NIV say to those with fearful hearts, "Be strong, do not fear; your God will come, he will come with vengeance; with divine retribution he will come to save you."

Isaiah 41:10 NIV So do not fear, for I am with you; do not be dismayed, for I am your God. I will strengthen you and help you; I will uphold you with my righteous right hand.

With any type of abuse there is an open door for fear to come in consume our lives. God's word stresses on the importance of not letting fear take over our lives. That is easier said than done. So how do we combat the spirit of fear? Immersing ourselves in the Word of God and soaking up His Holy Spirit. If your mindset is on the love of God then fear has to leave. Remember it's a spiritual battle.

Ephesians 6:10-18 (The Armor of God) NIV Finally, be strong in the Lord and in his mighty power. Put on the full armor of God, so that you can take your stand against the devil's schemes. For our struggle is not against flesh and blood, but against the rulers, against the authorities, against the powers of this dark world and against the spiritual forces of evil in the heavenly realms.

Prayer

Lord God of Heaven, please forgive me of anything in my past that I have done that has opened the door of shame to come into my life and cause me to feel ashamed. Help me to understand my worth in You and that I no longer have to be ashamed. Thank You, Lord, for Your Saving Grace. Amen.

Reflection

What am I ashamed of?

What secrets do I have that I would be ashamed of if someone found out?

Chapter 4

Fear

For God hath not given us the spirit of fear; but of power, and of love, and of a sound mind. (2 Timothy 1:7)NIV

We all fear something but a true spirit of fear can paralyze us into a place that we cannot move forward toward the destiny that God has set for us. Some of the fears the enemy tries to influence us with are fear of what people think, fear of being a failure and the fear that we will be stuck in our current situation forever.

When we fear what people think, it limits our ability to rise up over the very things that are trying to hold us down. We fear if we rise up after a fall of divorce that people will see us as not humble. If we are happy again and set free from the past there are people who will come against us trying to put doubt and shame on us again. We must stay in the word and rise above the shame and the fear.

The definition of fear is a distressing emotion aroused by impending danger, evil, pain, etc., whether the threat is real or imagined; the feeling or condition of being afraid.

Synonyms: foreboding, apprehension, consternation, dismay, dread, terror, fright, panic, horror, trepidation, qualm.

We have to recognize that the fear itself is the danger and the evil and causing us the pain and the Lord says we don't have to live in fear.

John 8:36 NIV So if the Son sets you free, you will be free indeed

Hallelujah! If I could reach out to every hurting woman of God and impart into her the true meaning of who she is in God and allow her to see she have nothing to fear I would. My heart cries out to God for healing and restoration of every wounded flower that God has created in His image

Another thing we fear is the fear of being in unfamiliar territory. Someone who has been abused, whether it is physical, sexual or emotional, has the fear of the unknown. When we chose to remove ourselves from the environment that is causing the abuse we have to face unknown possibilities and most people broken from abuse have been brainwashed by their abuser to believe that they cannot make it on their own, they can't survive without their abuser taking care of them. My second marriage was to a Christian man that was a Viet Nam Veteran who had Post Traumatic Stress Disorder and could not get his anger under control and struggled every day with a spiritual battle that we were not able at that time in our walk with the Lord to overcome. In order for me and my children to be safe, I left several times but always went back. Many people who have not been in that situation do not understand. Why would anyone go back? I hear that statement from people a lot. It's not that simple. My self-worth had been so conditioned to believe that I was the cause of his stress and anger that I had to go back and make it better. Domestic violence abusers go through a cycle of violence. They have a burst of violence and then they sincerely have thoughts of remorse and are really sorry .But when the victim forgives them and continues in the relationship it isn't long before the abuser starts to get angry again and have an episode of violence. The cycle goes around and around until someone breaks the cycle. They can get help and change if they realize their thought patterns are different from people who are not violent and they have to learn to act and re-act in a totally different manner than they have been programmed to and I believe without total surrender to the Lord and intervention of the power of the Holy Spirit to change the way their mind is, no amount of counseling is going to heal the cause of the dysfunction.

2 Corinthians 4:4 NIV The god of this age has blinded the minds of unbelievers, so that they cannot see the light of the gospel that displays the glory of Christ, who is the image of God.

Romans 12:2NIV Do not conform to the pattern of this world, but be transformed by the renewing of your mind. Then you will be able to test and approve what God's will is—his good, pleasing and perfect will.

Here is an excerpt from the Helpguide.org on Domestic Violence explaining the emotional abuse that occurs in domestic abuse situations.

"The aim of emotional abuse is to chip away at your feelings of self-worth and independence. If you're the victim of emotional abuse, you may feel that there is no way out of the relationship or that without your abusive partner you have nothing.

Emotional abuse includes verbal abuse such as yelling, name-calling, blaming, and shaming. Isolation, intimidation, and controlling behavior also fall under emotional abuse. Additionally, abusers who use emotional or psychological abuse often throw in threats of physical violence or other repercussions if you don't do what they want.

You may think that physical abuse is far worse than emotional abuse, since physical violence can send you to the hospital and leave you with scars. But, the scars of emotional abuse are very real, and they run deep. In fact, emotional abuse can be just as damaging as physical abuse—sometimes even more so."

In my situation my husband was sincerely sorry for his outbursts and the pattern of events was about a year apart which gave me time to forgive and believe that the situation was not going to happen again. Each incident escalated getting a little more violent each time to the point that I was seriously injured and I knew if I went back the next time he would probably kill me. The Lord spoke to me and said, "If you continue this relationship who is going to raise your children when the worst happens" The Lord gave me a vision of a bee hive.

He said if you put your hand in the bee hive you will get stung. So I saw myself getting attacked by bees and I quickly pulled my hand out of the bee hive and I was angry at the bees. The Lord said it's not the bees' fault, that s their nature. So I forgave the bees and forgot the danger and put my hand in the hive again expecting that since I had forgiven them they would not bite me again and they attacked my hand again. I pulled my hand out and was extremely angry that they had stung me again especially since I showed them grace and forgiveness. The Lord said to me, "whose fault is it yours or the bees that you were stung the second time? I told you it was their nature so you have no one to blame but yourself." So the lesson I learned was that I can forgive someone but if I continue to stay in a situation that is harmful then I am to blame. God always calls us to be wise.

There have been many misinterpretations of the scripture in the Bible that says God hates divorce. Usually it is used to keep a person in an abusive situation. Sometimes it is by the church because they have not prayerfully asked what the Lord meant in this situation. This is usually attached to a "religious spirit" that tries to keep the churches controlled and dominated by rules and not allow the Holy Spirit to have freedom in the church to produce fruit.

Malachi 2: 10NIV Do we not all have one Father? Did not one God create us? Why do we profane the covenant of our ancestors by being unfaithful to one another? 13 Another thing you do: You flood the Lord's altar with tears. You weep and wail because he no longer looks with favor on your offerings or accepts them with pleasure from your hands. 14 You ask, "Why?" It is because the Lord is the witness between you and the wife of your youth. You have been unfaithful to her, though she is your partner, the wife of your marriage covenant. 15 Has not the one God made you? You belong to him in body and spirit. And what does the one God seek? Godly offspring. So be on your guard, and do not be unfaithful to the wife of your youth. 16 "The man who hates and divorces his wife," says the Lord, the God of Israel, "does violence to the one he should protect," says the Lord Almighty. So be on your guard, and do not be unfaithful.

I had a revelation on this scripture when I was going through divorce and it was that being unfaithful does not necessarily mean with another person. A person can be unfaithful in their covenant to love and protect you, unfaithful by serving other gods such as money, pornography, and their own anger. If someone is not serving God then they are serving the enemy. It's that simple. Every single situation is different and the only way to get answers on what you need to do is to seek the Lord with all your heart and allow Him to guide you.

I know of many situations the Lord turned the situation around and the marriage was restored but this is something that happens when both people are willing to seek the Lord and to compromise and forgive and to recognize each parties part in the breakdown of the marriage.

In most abusive situations, the abuser is not going to be Kingdom minded and has shut out the still small voice of the Holy Spirit that keeps us from harming others. Abuse is the opposite of love and we are called to love one another.

What's important is that we don't allow these things from the past to stop us from moving forward in the way the Lord has planned for us. If you have been abused and/or divorced, let the past be the past and allow the Lord to make your present and future something beautiful.

Prayer

"Heavenly Father please touch me as I read these pages, let them come alive with life and allow my ears to be open, eyes to be open, mind to be open, heart to be open to receive what You have for me. Father, we know you did not give us the spirit of fear so we declare Matthew 6:10 Your kingdom come, Your will be done, on earth as it is in heaven. We speak life into those areas that we are fearful and ask that You fill us with the power of the Holy Spirit and give us peace, love and a sound mind. Thank you Lord. In Jesus Name Precious and Holy Name, Amen"

Reflection

What am I afraid of?

Are my fears unfounded?

What can I do step by step to conquer my fears?

Chapter 5

Unequally Yoked

Do not be yoked together with unbelievers. For what do righteousness and wickedness have in common? Or what fellowship can light have with darkness? 2Corinthians6:14 (NIV)

Someone I respect immensely in the evangelistic community calls being unequally yoked "attaching yourself to crazy". I had always had a tendency to be attracted to men that were like my father. I loved and adored my father but he was a very dominating person. I remember following him around with a tool belt, hammering things and fixing cars. He loved his cars and motorcycles. When I became about eleven or twelve years old my tomboyish ways were giving way to being a young woman and he could not handle that aspect of our relationship. He became withdrawn and really had nothing much to do with me. I have carried that rejection and have been attracted to men who were strong and dominating just like him. I seem to attract controlling men who really have no love or compassion for me as a person, they want me to take care of them completely but give nothing back in return. I have a tendency to fall into a caregiving mode and overlook the red flags telling me that the relationship is completely one sided.

In this process and journey of trying to make myself in the image of what God has called me to be I asked Him to show me what a good relationship is like. I began to start noticing those men around me that were actually good to their wives and cared about them as people. They nurtured who their wives are and encourage them to follow their dreams. The men are confident in who they are in the Lord so they are not threatened by their wives succeeding in the things the Lord has called them to. They actually see how their wives being fulfilled complete the relationship and make it whole. They are truly one in the Lord. When they have disagreements there is communication and compromise on both sides. I thank the Lord for allowing me to see these good examples around me.

Some of the issues that had to be dealt with in the situations where I was unequally yoked where major disagreements about things that are essential to my and my children's relationship with the Lord. Pornography, allowing other relationships to take priority over the covenant marriage relationship, ethical situations I couldn't be a part of, addictions, gambling, lying and arguing over abusive behavior of the children, were some of the issues I had to deal with. I have to say "all things DO work together for good" because out of these situations my prayer life and becoming an intercessor grew and matured. I learned so much about spiritual warfare and how to deal with these particular issues during the times of being under duress.

Being submissive is something I am good at, too good. But being submissive does not mean to lay down and take an emotional, verbal or physical beating just because your husband has a need to dominate you. I had to learn the balance and the difference between a man who makes wise decisions you can trust, and a man who makes foolish decisions and will not allow his wife to have any input into the decision making process. Men who dominate and control have self-esteem issues themselves and sometimes no matter how much you try and build them up they become resentful because they know in their hearts they are not living the way the Lord has called them to live. It's a no-win situation.

Ephesians 5:1-13(NIV) Follow God's example, therefore, as dearly loved children and walk in the way of love, just as Christ loved us and gave himself up for us as a fragrant offering and sacrifice to God. But among you there must not be even a hint of sexual immorality, or of any kind of impurity, or of greed, because these are improper for God's holy people. Nor should there be obscenity, foolish talk or coarse joking, which are out of place, but rather thanksgiving. For of this you can be sure: No immoral, impure or greedy person—such a person is an idolater—has any inheritance in the kingdom of Christ and of God. Let no one deceive you with empty words, for because of such things God's wrath comes on those who are disobedient. 7 Therefore do not be partners with them. For you were once darkness, but now you are light in the Lord. Live as children of light (for the fruit of the light consists in all goodness, righteousness and truth) and find out what pleases the Lord. Have nothing to do with the fruitless deeds of darkness, but rather expose them. It is shameful even to mention what the disobedient do in secret. But everything exposed by the light becomes visible—and everything that is illuminated becomes a light.

Ephesians 5:21-32(NIV) Submit to one another out of reverence for Christ. Wives, submit yourselves to your own husbands as you do to the Lord. For the husband is the head of the wife as Christ is the head of the church, his body, of which he is the Savior. Now as the church submits to Christ, so also wives should submit to their husbands in everything. Husbands, love your wives, just as Christ loved the church and gave himself up for her to make her holy, cleansing her by the washing with water through the word, and to present her to himself as a radiant church, without stain or wrinkle or any other blemish, but holy and blameless. In this same way, husbands ought to love their wives as their own bodies. He who loves his wife loves himself. After all, no one ever hated their own body, but they feed and care for their body, just as Christ does the church—for we are members of his body. "For this reason a man will leave his father and mother and be united to his wife, and the two will become one flesh." This is a profound mystery—but I am talking about Christ and the church. However, each one of you also must love his wife as he loves himself, and the wife must respect her husband.

We are created to respond to our husbands being the head of the household when they are in line with what the Lord wants them to do. It's easy for us to be comfortable and submissive when a man's priorities are right with the Lord. It doesn't mean they are perfect it just means that their heart is right with the Lord and when this happens it unleashes all the fruits of the Spirit into the marriage relationship and both husband and wife are satisfied.

Galatians 5:22-24(Amplified Bible) But the fruit of the [Holy] Spirit [the work which His presence within accomplishes] is love, joy (gladness), peace, patience (an even temper, forbearance), kindness, goodness (benevolence), faithfulness, Gentleness (meekness, humility), self-control (self-restraint, continence). Against such things there is no law that can bring a charge. And those who belong to Christ Jesus (the Messiah) have crucified the flesh (the godless human nature) with its passions and appetites and desires.

Sometimes we are already married to someone that is not walking with the Lord the way they should and the Bible speaks of this also. This is the time we must be tolerant and show unconditional love for those around us that have not yet come to the place of receiving Christ's blessings. If the marriage is healthy in the sense that there is no abuse then there is hope that with love and kindness an unbelieving husband will come to know the Lord. In the Old Testament the laws were explicit.

Deuteronomy13:6-10 NIV If your very own brother, or your son or daughter, or the wife you love, or your closest friend secretly entices you, saying, "Let us go and worship other gods" (gods that neither you nor your ancestors have known, gods of the peoples around you, whether near or far, from one end of the land to the other), do not yield to them or listen to them. Show them no pity. Do not spare them or shield them. You must certainly put them to death. Your hand must be the first in putting them to death, and then the hands of all the people. Stone them to death, because they tried to turn you away from the Lord your God, who brought you out of Egypt, out of the land of slavery.

Wow! So Harsh! Thank you Lord, that we don't live under the Old Testament rules and regulations, and that You sent Your Son to take our place on the cross. Thank You Jesus for making the ultimate sacrifice for me and dying for me so I would be forgiven and allowed to move forward in freedom and Your Grace and Mercy.

Obviously the Lord is really serious about serving Him and only Him so what do we do if we are unequally yoked. I believe if your spouse is an unbeliever you can win them over by your gentle spirit and showing your spouse the true meaning of this scripture.

Galatians 5:22 22(NIV) But the fruit of the Spirit is love, joy, peace, forbearance, kindness, goodness, faithfulness, 23 gentleness and self-control. Against such things there is no law.

By thanking the Lord for their good qualities and constantly being in the Lord's presence by worship and praise I believe the unbeliever will be saved. Delay in the answer to our prayers is not necessarily a denial from the Lord. You also cannot judge the situation by looking at what you see in the natural realm. There is such a vast difference between the natural and the spiritual we must always have our Holy Spirit filtered glasses on to see what is happening in the Spiritual Realm. This is a simple but effective prayer.

Matthew6:9-10(NIV) "This, then, is how you should pray: " 'Our Father in heaven, hallowed be your name, your kingdom come, your will be done, on earth as it is in heaven.'"

2 Corinthians 4:1-6(NIV) Therefore, since through God's mercy we have this ministry, we do not lose heart. Rather, we have renounced secret and shameful ways; we do not use deception, nor do we distort the word of God. On the contrary, by setting forth the truth plainly we commend ourselves to everyone's conscience in the sight of God. And even if our gospel is veiled, it is veiled to those who are perishing. The god of this age has blinded the minds of unbelievers, so that they cannot see the light of the gospel that displays the glory of Christ, who is the image of God. For what we preach is not ourselves, but Jesus Christ as Lord, and ourselves as your servants for Jesus' sake. For God, who said, "Let light shine out of darkness," made his light shine in our hearts to give us the light of the knowledge of God's glory displayed in the face of Christ.

1 Corinthians 7:12-16 (NIV) To the rest I say this (I, not the Lord): If any brother has a wife who is not a believer and she is willing to live with him, he must not divorce her. And if a woman has a husband who is not a believer and he is willing to live with her, she must not divorce him. For the unbelieving husband has been sanctified through his wife, and the unbelieving wife has been sanctified through her believing husband. Otherwise your children would be unclean, but as it is, they are holy. But if the unbeliever leaves, let it be so. The brother or the sister is not bound in such circumstances; God has called us to live in peace. How do you know, wife, whether you will save your husband? Or, how do you know, husband, whether you will save your wife?

So whatever your situation is, please, please and I say again, bathe your situation in prayer before you make decisions. Seek the Lord's will in the situation. Ask Him for wisdom and to show you what is right with your family. I believe there are no pat answers, no quick fixes, no "ten ways to fix your marriage". I believe that every situation is unique in its own way and without seeking the Lord and allowing Him to guide you; you leave yourself open to the possibilities of failure.

Philippians 4:8 (NIV)Finally, brethren, whatsoever things are true, whatsoever things are honest, whatsoever things are just, whatsoever things are pure, whatsoever things are lovely, whatsoever things are of good report; if there be any virtue, and if there be any praise, think on these things.

Prayer

I pray that the eyes of my heart may be enlightened in order that I may know the hope to which You have called me, the riches of Your glorious inheritance and Your incomparably great power for us who believe.

Reflection

Am I in a relationship that is unequally yoked?

How can I pray for my spouse and show him/her support?

How can I be a Proverbs 31 wife either now or for future relationships?

Chapter 6

Adultery

"You shall not commit adultery. (Deuteronomy 5:18)NIV

We see it everywhere. The thrill of having a secret relationship with someone has been portrayed as something exciting and thrilling. It is prevalent in everything we see on television and everything we read. Adultery is one issue no one wants to have to go through. If you have given your trust to someone and they betray you and give their affections to someone else it can be devastating. This is a form of victimization also and the good news is that healing is possible.

The statistics of adultery in the United States is staggering. According to a website Truthaboutdeception.com and the researchers Buss & Shackelford, 30 to 60% will engage in infidelity during the course of their marriage. And the most disturbing statistics are 2 to 3% of all children born are born from a union during infidelity. It is so devastating. It does not only affect the two people, it affects the whole dynamic of the family unit. This was not God's design for marriage. We are to be faithful and to pass on to our future generations the blessings of the Lord to further the Kingdom.

Emotional adultery is as devastating as the physical cheating. When a spouse has another person in their life that is their "best friend" or companion that they share all the things that they should be sharing in the marriage exclusively, the devastation is as bad if not worse than a real affair. The feelings of betrayal and the damage are very real.

I would be amiss if I didn't talk about the other side. A subject we need to cover if we are going to talk about adultery is what if you were the one who committed adultery? Can there be healing for you too? Of course, forgiveness from the Lord covers all of our sins and in order to get healing you must confess your sins to the Lord, sincerely recognize what you had done that was in error according to the Word, and then the most important thing-forgive yourself. You have to soak in the Holy Spirit and allow God's forgiveness to wash over you and move on and put the past behind you. You need to prayerfully try to understand the root behind the adultery and see if there is anything in your past that could cause you to look to someone other than your spouse for affection. A lot of times, there is something underlying in your heart that needs healing. Many of the different abuses that could happen to us can cause us to be weak in areas and cause us to fall.

The story of King David and Bathsheba is a good example of falling short of what God calls us to be and the power of restoration.

2 Samuel 11:1-5 In the spring, at the time when kings go off to war, David sent Joab out with the king's men and the whole Israelite army. They destroyed the Ammonites and besieged Rabbah. But David remained in Jerusalem. One evening David got up from his bed and walked around on the roof of the palace. From the roof he saw a woman bathing. The woman was very beautiful, and David sent someone to find out about her. The man said, "She is Bathsheba, the daughter of Eliam and the wife of Uriah the Hittite." Then David sent messengers to get her. She came to him, and he slept with her. (Now she was purifying herself from her monthly uncleanness.) Then she went back home. The woman conceived and sent word to David, saying, "I am pregnant."

We all know the story. David committed adultery with Bathsheba and then when she became pregnant King David made plans to have her husband murdered in order to cover up the sin. Sex, lies and murder, all because he didn't flee when he was gazing at Bathsheba from his roof. The enemy comes in with a mere thought and acting on that one thought can succumb to a spiral downward fall in your life to devastating effects. Remember the enemy comes to steal, kill and destroy.

John 10:10 The thief comes only to steal and kill and destroy; I have come that they may have life, and have it to the full.

Hebrews 13:4 (NIV) Marriage should be honored by all, and the marriage bed kept pure, for God will judge the adulterer and all the sexually immoral.

But adultery is not the unforgivable sin. There can be restoration and healing after adultery. Marriages and relationships through the power of the Holy Spirit can be restored and stronger than ever.

So be on your guard if you know you are weak in this area. Ask the Lord to show you the areas and the traps that can cause you to fall. If pornography and the Internet are a problem then don't go there. If there is someone else in your life that you feel attracted to then flee, don't go there.

Stay away from them physically. Don't have work lunches with members of the opposite sex alone. Guard your heart and don't give the enemy a foothold in your life. I know this is harder than it sounds. Sometimes you need someone you can be accountable to, and to help you with encouragement. Seek out wise counsel from those you trust and pray, pray, pray. Take one step at a time. Every time you turn away from the things that try to trap you, no matter how hard it is to stay clear of the things that distract you, you have won against the enemy. Each time you make a small step forward you are making progress in the spiritual realm and taking back territory from the enemy. If you fail and give in then pick yourself up and ask God for forgiveness and resolve that it is a new day, forgive yourself, and move forward. Each step will bring you closer to deliverance.

Ephesians 5:3(NIV) But among you there must not be even a hint of sexual immorality, or of any kind of impurity, or of greed, because these are improper for God's holy people.

Proverbs 4:23(NIV) Above all else, guard your heart, for everything you do flows from it.

Philippians 4:7(NIV) And the peace of God, which transcends all understanding, will guard your hearts and your minds in Christ Jesus.

It's a lot harder than it sounds but with diligence we can all allow the mind of Christ and all goodness to take over in our lives. Just remember where there is truth there is freedom. When we allow ourselves to test those boundaries bordering on entertaining thoughts even briefly of someone else besides our spouse, we get caught up in bondage. We are living with emotions of guilt, shame, trying to keep a secret, fear, etc. and they all have the same effect on our lives and that is to distract us from our true calling. Sometimes this means physically not placing ourselves in situations that could bring temptation. If we are obedient and resist temptation, the enemy will run because he has no open door to torment us through. So just don't go there!

James 4:7(NIV) Submit yourselves, then, to God. Resist the devil, and he will flee from you.

Prayer

Heavenly Father, we pray that any residual effects of adultery that have wreaked havoc on our relationships have to come under Your healing. Show us if we are guilty in any of these areas and help us to bring all thoughts captive to Your Spirit. Please forgive us of any wrong doing and heal our broken hearts of any wrong doing committed against us. Thank You Lord.

Reflection

Have I been betrayed by adultery?

How can I take steps to forgive?

Have I been unfaithful?

How can I take steps to forgive myself and move forward in the plans God has for me?

Chapter 7

Counseling

"For where two or three gather in my name, there am I with them." Matthew 18:20NIV

SHOULD YOU GO TO FORMAL COUNSELING? THIS is going to be an individual decision that you will have to make prayerfully. I have mixed feelings of going to counseling. I sometimes have a tendency to want to do things on my own and I believe with the power of the Holy Spirit we can overcome any obstacles we have in our lives. But I also believe that there are times we need wise counsel to make decisions because we might be clouded with emotions and not thinking clearly. I had a bad experience and a good experience with counseling. In one relationship that was failing, we sought counseling but when one party won't acknowledge a need for counseling and try and work on the marriage, it can be a very confusing time for the one who is being victimized.

Here are some red flags that counseling is not working.

1. One person in the relationship will not open up and actively participate. The counselor can only work on helping the relationship if he/she knows the true situation.

2. The counselor takes one person's side. The counselor has to be

unbiased and deal with both spouses equally. In one situation my spouse became friends outside the counseling sessions as a close personal friend with the counselor. The counselor began accepting favors from my spouse. This was completely unethical on the counselor's part and I felt betrayed not only by my spouse but the counselor. I no longer felt safe sharing my feelings or issues.

3. The counselor lets one spouse dominate the other. He/she lets each other cut the other off or speak for each other. Each person needs to have their own speech and freedom during the sessions.

4. The counselor does not discuss certain ground rules for the sessions. Basic ground rules such as common sense courtesy and base line respect for each person is a necessity.

5. The counselor is judgmental and makes you uncomfortable about the issues you are sharing.

6. The counselor seems to be overly emotional when hearing your issues and/or they try and push you into some type of therapy you are not comfortable with.

In a nutshell a good counselor will be a mediator, trying to help each side their weaknesses and their strengths. Also giving positive feedback and encouraging each person to grow in the relationship and try to get the issues resolved for both parties. I had a positive experience with a Pastor counselor where he was gentle and nonjudgmental toward both my spouse and I. He gave us positive homework to work on in reflecting on the basics of having a good relationship.

Here are some basic guidelines to consider in choosing a counselor.

1. Ask about the counselor's credentials, make sure they are meeting all the licensing requirements for both federal and local guidelines.

2. They are willing to discuss with you their experience in your particular need for counseling.

3. They and their staff always exhibit the utmost professionalism. Confidentiality is so important for you to feel you are in a safe environment in order to be able to discuss the most intimate personal issues you may have.

4. A good counselor continues to be focused on you making progress without pushing you to fast if you aren't ready.

5. Ask around to your friends and family, if people you know are comfortable with a particular counselor, you might also be comfortable.

What does the Word say about counseling? There are many scriptures concerning seeking wise counsel and seeking the Lord's wisdom in situations.

Psalm 1:1 (NIV) Blessed is the one who does not walk in step with the wicked or stand in the way that sinners take or sit in the company of mockers, but whose delight is in the law of the Lord, and who meditates on his law day and night.

John 14: 15-17 (NIV) "If you love me, keep my commands. And I will ask the Father, and he will give you another advocate to help you and be with you forever, the Spirit of truth. The world cannot accept him, because it neither sees him nor knows him. But you know him, for he lives with you and will be in you.

John 14:25-27 (NIV) "All this I have spoken while still with you. But the Advocate, the Holy Spirit, whom the Father will send in my name, will teach you all things and will remind you of everything I have said to you. Peace I leave with you; my peace I give you. I do not give to you as the world gives. Do not let your hearts be troubled and do not be afraid.

When Jesus was leaving this earth He said he was sending His Spirit of Truth to abide with us to teach us all things and give us wise counsel and comfort.

John14: 13 (NIV)But when he, the Spirit of truth, comes, he will guide you into all the truth. He will not speak on his own; he will speak only what he hears, and he will tell you what is yet to come. 14 He will glorify me because it is from me that he will receive what he will make known to you. 15 All that belongs to the Father is mine. That is why I said the Spirit will receive from me what he will make known to you."

Psalms 73:21-26 (NIV) When my heart was grieved and my spirit embittered, I was senseless and ignorant; I was a brute beast before you. Yet I am always with you; you hold me by my right hand. You guide me with your counsel, and afterward you will take me into glory. Whom have I in heaven but you? And earth has nothing I desire besides you. My flesh and my heart may fail, but God is the strength of my heart and my portion forever.

There are times when we are so overcome with emotions that we cannot hear clearly what the Spirit is telling us. This is the time that we may need to seek wise counsel from those we can trust.

Job's friends were his worst enemies when he was going through trials and they discouraged him and gave bad advice so be careful who you share your problems with. Even your closest friends sometimes can't see clearly the situation. They may give you well-meaning advice but not necessarily within the Lord's will for your life.

Job 38: 1-2 (NIV) Then the Lord spoke to Job out of the storm. He said: "Who is this that obscures my plans with words without knowledge?

Look for friends carefully to share your issues with and seek wise counsel. Not everyone has the maturity in the Lord or the presence of mind to give you wise and Godly advice.

Job 42:1-3 (NIV)Then Job replied to the Lord: "I know that you can do all things; no purpose of yours can be thwarted. You asked, 'Who is this that obscures my plans without knowledge?' Surely I spoke of things I did not understand, things too wonderful for me to know.

Prayer

Lord Jesus, thank you for sending the Spirit of Truth to counsel, guide and comfort me in my times of need. I ask that you show me how to move close to the Holy Spirit and breathe in His Presence to help me make wise decisions in my life. I give Him free reign over my life. In Jesus Name.

Reflection

Does my situation call for professional counseling?

Can I resolve these issues with prayer and communication with my spouse?

Do I need counseling in order to think clearly on some issues that seem clouded in my emotions?

Chapter 8

Who Are We?

See what great love the Father has lavished on us, that we should be called children of God! And that is what we are! The reason the world does not know us is that it did not know him. (1 John 3:1)NIV

For those who are led by the Spirit of God are the children of God. (Romans 8:14)NIV

WHO ARE WE AND WHY ARE WE here? This is the age old question that has caused so much discussion and confusion. The answer is simple. We are the children of the living God.

Romans 8:17 NIV Now if we are children, then we are heirs—heirs of God and co-heirs with Christ, if indeed we share in his sufferings in order that we may also share in his glory.

We are heirs to the throne of God. We are created by the Lord.

Psalm 139:14 NIV I praise you because I am fearfully and wonderfully made; your works are wonderful, I know that full well.

We are created in His image.

Genesis 1:27 NIV So God created mankind in his own image, in the image of God he created them; male and female he created them.

We are chosen for a greater purpose.

Deuteronomy 7:6 NIV For you are a people holy to the LORD your God. The LORD your God has chosen you out of all the peoples on the face of the earth to be his people, his treasured possession.

Ephesians 1:3-14 Praise be to the God and Father of our Lord Jesus Christ, who has blessed us in the heavenly realms with every spiritual blessing in Christ. For he chose us in him before the creation of the world to be holy and blameless in his sight. In love he predestined us for adoption to sonship through Jesus Christ, in accordance with his pleasure and will to the praise of his glorious grace, which he has freely given us in the One he loves. In him we have redemption through his blood, the forgiveness of sins, in accordance with the riches of God's grace that he lavished on us. With all wisdom and understanding, he made known to us the mystery of his will according to his good pleasure, which he purposed in Christ, to be put into effect when the times reach their fulfillment—to bring unity to all things in heaven and on earth under Christ. In him we were also chosen, having been predestined according to the plan of him who works out everything in conformity with the purpose of his will, in order that we, who were the first to put our hope in Christ, might be for the praise of his glory. And you also were included in Christ when you heard the message of truth, the gospel of your salvation. When you believed, you were marked in him with a seal, the promised Holy Spirit, who is a deposit guaranteeing our inheritance until the redemption of those who are God's possession—to the praise of his glory.

I have grown up entertaining a wrong idea of who I really was based on the things that had happened to me as a child. Molestation has a way of opening doors to the enemy to cause you to see yourself differently than the Lord sees you in order to distract you from your true calling. It took years of healing and affirmation from the Lord before it really sunk in, of who I really am. I started asking the Lord in my prayer life to show me who I was. He showed me things about my heritage both physical and spiritual. In the natural I learned that I am a descendant of the Jewish people. This was exciting to me to learn I really had the bloodlines of God's chosen people. In the spiritual realm the Lord showed me I was a descendant of the Tribe of Benjamin. Is this important in the natural who we are? Yes definitely. The Lord has a plan and every detail of your life has been predestined and ordained by the Lord. Look at how many genealogies there are in the Bible. You know the tedious readings of so and so begot so and so and they go on forever. The Lord would not include these in His Word if it weren't so important to Him.

John 4:9 (NIV) The Samaritan woman said to him, "You are a Jew and I am a Samaritan woman. How can you ask me for a drink?" (For Jews do not associate with Samaritans.)

The Samaritan woman knew she was from a different culture and should not be talking to Jesus and she know she could be trouble with her peers and His people by talking to Him. He talked to her anyway. He saw her as the person God had created her to be, not as the woman with all the limitations that her culture and her past had put on her. Jesus sees us as we are and accepts us anyway. He can forgive all of our past and heal all of our hurts and allow us to live freely as God the Father has called us to live. We are called to a certain predestined role and we need to seek God and ask Him to show us what our destiny is and how to move forward and fulfill it.

Jeremiah 29:11 NIV For I know the plans I have for you," declares the Lord, "plans to prosper you and not to harm you, plans to give you hope and a future.

What else do I know about myself? I have a gift of administration and also writing. Creativity flows from my very inner being. Painting, sketching and crafts these are all gifts the Lord has given to me to use for His Glory. It is exciting to explore each gifting and seek His will on how to use them to further the Kingdom.

James 1:17 NIV Every good and perfect gift is from above, coming down from the Father of the heavenly lights, who does not change like shifting shadows.

Prayer

Holy Spirit, Thank You, for being my comforter and being with me always. Help me to understand and grasp the reality of who I am in Christ. I want to stand up and take my rightful place free from pain, hurts and a broken heart. I want to feel the freedom so I can go out and show Your healing power to others. In Jesus Precious Healing Name. Amen.

Reflection

Who are my ancestors?

What gifts do I have?

How can I understand and enhance the gifts the Lord gave me?

Chapter 9

Stand up and Take your Rightful Place

Now if we are children, then we are heirs—heirs of God and co-heirs with Christ, if indeed we share in his sufferings in order that we may also share in his glory. Romans 8:17(NIV)

If you belong to Christ, then you are Abraham's seed, and heirs according to the promise.

Galatians 3:28-29(NIV)

SO HOW DO WE GET PAST THE mindset that we have that has been tainted by our past and the hurts that come against us? We have to know who we are. The only way to know who we are is to get as close to the Lord that we can in a personal intimate way. Understanding who Christ is can help us understand who we are.

I remember one time I was praying and begging the Lord for something. I was crying and must have looked pretty pathetic if anyone had seen me. I had a tendency to be pretty dramatic. The Lord spoke to me very clearly and said, "Why do you crawl around on your hands and knees under my Throne begging for crumbs? Stand up and take your rightful place as daughter of the King. Come boldly into my Throne room and ask Me what you will and I will answer You." Wow! Did I feel embarrassed picturing myself crawling around instead of standing upright and taking hold of my inheritance given to me by the Lord.

I had always suffered with crippling shyness until I began understanding who I am in the Lord. I was so shy that I would intentionally get straight A's in elementary and high school so when it came time to give an oral report I could decline and take an F and it didn't affect my grades that badly. I was terrified of embarrassing myself. Thoughts of falling down or saying something and being made fun of would permeate my thoughts and I was rendered helpless in fear. One day the Lord spoke to me and said, "Are you going to allow your shyness to stop you from serving Me? What if I tell you to go speak a word of knowledge or wisdom to someone who really needs to hear it and you refuse to go because you are fearful? I say to you that this is a form of unbelief, that you could be saved and sanctified by Me by the blood My Son shed for you and the blood was shed in vain for you if you cannot believe I am bigger than your shyness. This is being completely self-absorbed and selfish and you will have to put aside your fears and shyness to move forward into the calling I have for you." Talk about being chastised! Thank you Lord, I had not seen this side of it. I am so thankful that I do have the personal relationship with the Lord that He can talk to me and correct me. For those that are unbelievers or question my ability to hear the Lord I can only say that in my own thought process I would not have been able to come up with this analysis of my weakness all by myself. I was so consumed with fear that this thought could not have come from my little fearful brain. I love when a Revelation comes to me from the Lord.

On a lighter note along this same subject, I remember one time I was lying on the bed, dramatically crying and begging God for a particular answer in prayer and I had a Revelation of a picture of the Lord standing there with His arms crossed and His foot tapping patiently and He was saying, "Are you through yet? May we get on with what we need to do here?" I had to laugh at myself, it was so true.

Romans 8:17(NIV) Now if we are children, then we are heirs—heirs of God and co-heirs with Christ, if indeed we share in his sufferings in order that we may also share in his glory.

I Thessalonians 4-6 (NIV)For we know, brothers and sisters loved by God, that he has chosen you, because our gospel came to you not simply with words but also with power, with the Holy Spirit and deep conviction. You know how we lived among you for your sake. You became imitators of us and of the Lord, for you welcomed the message in the midst of severe suffering with the joy given by the Holy Spirit.

John 1:12-13(NIV) Yet to all who did receive him, to those who believed in his name, he gave the right to become children of God—children born not of natural descent, nor of human decision or a husband's will, but born of God.

Romans 8:19(NIV) For the creation waits in eager expectation for the children of God to be revealed.

Romans 8:2(NIV) that the creation itself will be liberated from its bondage to decay and brought into the freedom and glory of the children of God.

Romans 9:8(NIV) In other words, it is not the children by physical descent who are God's children, but it is the children of the promise who are regarded as Abraham's offspring.

Galatians 3:25-27 (NIV) Now that this faith has come, we are no longer under a guardian. So in Christ Jesus you are all children of God through faith, 27 for all of you who were baptized into Christ have clothed yourselves with Christ.

We are entering a new season with the Lord where we need to move forward and be obedient to Him at all cost. It is time to jump into the middle of the stream of Living Water instead of hanging out at the edge in the dirty stagnant pools. Peoples' lives are at stake. If we don't bring the good news who will?

Matthew 22: 14 (KJV) For many are called, but few are chosen.

So let's be the chosen and step up and take our place where we belong serving the One and Only Lord.

Prayer

Heavenly Father, I pray that the eyes of my heart may be enlightened in order that I may know the hope You have called me, the riches of Your glorious inheritance in Your holy people, and Your incomparably great power for us who believe. That power is the same as the mighty strength You exerted when You raised Christ from the dead and seated Him at Your right hand in the heavenly realms, far above all rule and authority, power and dominion, and every name that is invoked, not only in the present age but also in the one to come. And You placed all things under His feet and appointed Him to be head over everything for the church, which is His body, the fullness of Him who fills everything in every way.

Reflection

What steps can I take to make sure I am moving forward each day in the Lord?

Chapter 10

Prayer

"This, then, is how you should pray: "'Our Father in heaven, hallowed be your name, your kingdom come, your will be done, on earth as it is in heaven. Give us today our daily bread. ...

Matthew 6:8-14(NIV)

So how do we get from the point of being a victim to an overcomer? There are several key things we need to incorporate into our lives on a daily basis. The first is to acknowledge that you need Jesus to be your Savor and ask forgiveness for your sins. Once you have done this begin to pray, study God's Word and continually praise the Lord for the good things in your life and you will see a breakthrough and you will be an overcomer.

Praying is essential to opening up the communication with our Lord. If you spend time seeking Him and developing a relationship with Him you will learn who the Lord is and in essence you will learn who you are in Him.

So how do we pray? Just simply talk to the Lord. You don't need to know Biblical terms or perfect grammar, you just need to be yourself. There isn't anything that the Lord doesn't know already. He has big shoulders and unconditional love so if you need to cry out to the Lord with things you can't share with anyone else, He understands.

Matthew 6:9-13(NIV) "This, then, is how you should pray: "Our Father in heaven, hallowed be your name, your kingdom come, your will be done, on earth as it is in heaven. Give us today our daily bread. And forgive us our debts, as we also have forgiven our debtors. And lead us not into temptation, but deliver us from the evil one.

- Our Father in heaven, yes He is in Heaven watching over us.
- Hallowed be thy Name. The definition of hallowed is: holy, consecrated, sacred, and revered.
- Your Kingdom come, yes Lord, send Your Kingdom and all the power of Your love into our lives.
- Your Will be done. Praying for His perfect Will to consume our lives. His perfect Will is the best path for us.
- On earth as it is in Heaven. Praying down Heaven into our immediate circumstances.
- Give us our daily bread. Asking for our daily necessities and acknowledging we need Him. He knows what we need but by asking.

John 16:24(NIV) Until now you have not asked for anything in my name. Ask and you will receive, and your joy will be complete.

- And forgive us our debts. Asking for forgiveness for our daily shortcomings.
- As we forgive our debtors. There is a condition for our weaknesses to be forgiven and that is we must also forgive those who wrong us.

- And lead us not into temptation. Help us to keep on the right path that the Lord has ordained for us.

- But deliver us from the evil one. Praying for protection for us and our family and friends from the enemy.

In our society today we want everything described to us in the short version. I don't believe there is one formula we can follow to get results from our prayers. I believe that every situation in our lives is going to take different prayers and needs to be bathed in the Word. Our prayer life is a reflection of our relationship with God the Father.

1 Thessalonians 5:16-18 (NIV) Rejoice always, pray continually, give thanks in all circumstances; for this is God's will for you in Christ Jesus.

1 Kings 8:28(NIV) Yet give attention to your servant's prayer and his plea for mercy, LORD my God. Hear the cry and the prayer that your servant is praying in your presence this day.

1 Kings 9:3 (NIV) The LORD said to him: "I have heard the prayer and plea you have made before me; I have consecrated this temple, which you have built, by putting my Name there forever. My eyes and my heart will always be there.

Job 42:10 (NIV) After Job had prayed for his friends, the LORD restored his fortunes and gave him twice as much as he had before.

Psalm 39:12 (NIV) "Hear my prayer, LORD, listen to my cry for help; do not be deaf to my weeping. I dwell with you as a foreigner, a stranger, as all my ancestors were.

Mark 11:24 (NIV) Therefore I tell you, whatever you ask for in prayer, believe that you have received it, and it will be yours.

Mark 11:25 (NIV) And when you stand praying, if you hold anything against anyone, forgive them, so that your Father in heaven may forgive you your sins."

Sometimes when I pray for a specific person I ask the Lord to show me in some way how my prayers were answered. The Lord honors those prayers by allowing me to see the results, sometimes even years later.

If you don't know what to pray, pick up the Bible and pray according to His Word. His Word does not go out without accomplishing what its purpose is.

Isaiah 55:11(NIV) so is my word that goes out from my mouth: It will not return to me empty, but will accomplish what I desire and achieve the purpose for which I sent it.

One of my favorite prayers is the prayer that Jabez prayed.

I Chronicle4:10(NIV) Jabez cried out to the God of Israel, "Oh, that you would bless me and enlarge my territory! Let your hand be with me, and keep me from harm so that I will be free from pain." And God granted his request.

And God granted his request. AMEN!

Prayer

Help me Father to continually lift up Your Name in my life. Show me how to pray and to have a continual conversation with You daily. I want to build a relationship with You, not just make requests from You. I want to be so intimate with You that prayer is continually on my lips. I love You Lord.

Reflection

How can I have a more effective prayer life?

CHAPTER 11

PRAISE AND WORSHIP

Praise the Lord.
Praise God in his sanctuary;
praise him in his mighty heavens.
Praise him for his acts of power;
praise him for his surpassing greatness.
Praise him with the sounding of the trumpet,
praise him with the harp and lyre,
praise him with timbrel and dancing,
praise him with the strings and pipe,
praise him with the clash of cymbals,
praise him with resounding cymbals.
Let everything that has breath praise the Lord.
Praise the Lord. Psalms 150 (NIV)

THE DEFINITIONS OF PRAISE IS TO EXPRESS approval or admiration of; commend; extol.;to offer grateful homage to (God or a deity), as in words or song. I can think of times when I was alone and did not know God. As I look back I see how His hand has guided me even when I didn't know He was watching over me. How many times can you think of that time you had a "near miss" or a moment when you knew what just happened was an intervention of something unexplainable and you knew the situation should have gone a different direction. If you have a hard time remembering good times in your life, ask God to bring to remembrance and He surely will.

Praising the Lord can be exhibited in many different ways. Keeping a cheerful attitude continually and dwelling on positive things, not negative things, in dealing with people on a daily basis. It might take some practice changing your mind to praise the Lord but it will come easier with time. When you see situations ask the Lord to show you the good in it or how He is working in the situation. When there are people who rub you the wrong way ask the Lord to show you the positive and what lesson can be learned from the person. We can't always see what He is doing in the natural but He can show us what is happening in spiritual realms. When we come against difficult situations, having faith that God's will is going to prevail and that the outcome is for our growth is of utmost importance.

Hebrews 11:1-12 (NIV) Now faith is confidence in what we hope for and assurance about what we do not see. This is what the ancients were commended for.

By faith we understand that the universe was formed at God's command, so that what is seen was not made out of what was visible.

By faith Abel brought God a better offering than Cain did. By faith he was commended as righteous, when God spoke well of his offerings. And by faith Abel still speaks, even though he is dead.

By faith Enoch was taken from this life, so that he did not experience death: "He could not be found, because God had taken him away." For before he was taken, he was commended as one who pleased God. 6 And without faith it is impossible to please God, because anyone who comes to him must believe that he exists and that he rewards those who earnestly seek him.

By faith Noah, when warned about things not yet seen, in holy fear built an ark to save his family. By his faith he condemned the world and became heir of the righteousness that is in keeping with faith.

By faith Abraham, when called to go to a place he would later receive as his inheritance, obeyed and went, even though he did not know where he was going. By faith he made his home in the promised land like a stranger in a foreign country; he lived in tents, as did Isaac and Jacob, who were heirs with him of the same promise. For he was looking forward to the city with foundations, whose architect and builder is God. And by faith even Sarah, who was past childbearing age, was enabled to bear children because she considered him faithful who had made the promise. And so from this one man, and he as good as dead, came descendants as numerous as the stars in the sky and as countless as the sand on the seashore.

It's easy to praise the Lord when we have faith in who He is.

Philippians 3:8-9 (NIV) What is more, I consider everything a loss because of the surpassing worth of knowing Christ Jesus my Lord, for whose sake I have lost all things. I consider them garbage, that I may gain Christ and be found in him, not having a righteousness of my own that comes from the law, but that which is through faith in Christ—the righteousness that comes from God on the basis of faith.

My favorite way to praise the Lord actively and worship Him is through music. I surround myself with praise and worship music. I praise Him every minute and try to always show myself as in a state of praise to Him because without Him who knows where I would be. I find myself humming along in the grocery store to my favorite worship songs. You never know the effect of your attitude can have on the people around you. I had a conversation with one of my children and we were talking about the dark times we went through and I asked him what he remembered about the situation and he said he just remembers me singing all the time. I don't remember singing all the time but the Lord remembers and He brought me through some really tough times. I praise Him for that.

Music, dance, flagging, singing, and shouting to the Lord, these are wonderful ways to show praise the Lord. I enjoy just spending time with My Savior alone and soaking in His love and absorbing what He wants me to learn for the day. Setting aside a specific time and place to actively show praise is a good way to get into the habit of praising the Lord. Play some of your favorite praise music and sing along and concentrate on the Lord and tell Him how wonderful He is.

Jesus spoke to the woman at the well about worship.

John 4:21-23(NIV) "Woman," Jesus replied, "believe me, a time is coming when you will worship the Father neither on this mountain nor in Jerusalem. You Samaritans worship what you do not know; we worship what we do know, for salvation is from the Jews. Yet a time is coming and has now come when the true worshipers will worship the Father in the Spirit and in truth, for they are the kind of worshipers the Father seeks.

I find if I do not stay in a state of praise and worship I start to forget the promises the Lord has given me on who I am and my worth to Him so it is a double edged sword. It builds me up also when I worship the Father. I am so much more prepared to meet the obstacles that come against me when I am consumed in worshiping the one true God.

Philippians 4:4(NIV) Rejoice in the Lord always. I will say it again: Rejoice!

Prayer

Thank You Lord, I praise You for all things work together for good for me because I am called according to Your purpose. I will rejoice in every situation because even if I don't understand what is happening in the natural I know You are in control on earth as You are in Heaven. I love You Lord. Amen.

Reflection

What areas in my life do I fall short in praising God for?

CHAPTER 12

GLORY!

The heavens declare the glory of God; the skies proclaim the work of his hands. Psalms 19:1(NIV)

SOMETHING HAPPENS WHEN WE SPEND TIME IN prayer, praise and studying the Word of God. There is a supernatural manifestation where God's glory rests on our lives. If we surrender and allow Him to consume our lives and give over everything to His purpose, something wonderful happens and His Glory falls.

The definition of Glory is:

- very great praise honor or distinction bestowed by common consent
- renown something that is a source of honor fame or admiration an object of pride
- adoring praise or worshipful thanksgiving
- resplendent beauty or magnificence the glory
- a state of great splendor or prosperity
- a state of absolute happiness gratification

- the splendor and bliss of heaven
- to exult with triumph rejoice proudly

When we praise, worship and honor our Lord something amazing happens. The Lord turns our situations around and sends His Glory and imparts gifts, miracles and blessings that we have not even imagined we were worthy to receive. He releases the splendor and bliss of heaven and He triumphs and rejoices proudly of who we are and all Heaven rejoices with Him! How wonderful it is that we can come to Him and He can show us so much mercy, grace and love.

Philippians 4:19(KJV) But my God shall supply all your need according to his riches in glory by Christ Jesus.

In the Glory we find our resources for the very basics of living. God supplies us with more than enough.

Deuteronomy 5:24 (NIV) And you said, "The Lord our God has shown us his glory and his majesty, and we have heard his voice from the fire. Today we have seen that a person can live even if God speaks with them. Psalm 19:1(NIV) The heavens declare the glory of God; the skies proclaim the work of his hands.

Psalm 29:3(NIV) The voice of the LORD is over the waters; the God of glory thunders, the LORD thunders over the mighty waters.

Psalm 63:11 (NIV) But the king will rejoice in God; all who swear by God will glory in him, while the mouths of liars will be silenced.

Notice the power of Glory, it thunders and silences the mouths of liars.

Psalm 79:9 (NIV) Help us, God our Savior, for the glory of your name; deliver us and forgive our sins for your name's sake.

Ezekiel 43: 1-3 (NIV)Then the man brought me to the gate facing east, and I saw the glory of the God of Israel coming from the east. His voice was like the roar of rushing waters, and the land was radiant with his glory. The vision

I saw was like the vision I had seen when he came to destroy the city and like the visions I had seen by the Kebar River, and I fell facedown.

John 11:40 (NIV) Then Jesus said, "Did I not tell you that if you believe, you will see the glory of God?"

Acts 7:55 (NIV) But Stephen, full of the Holy Spirit, looked up to heaven and saw the glory of God, and Jesus standing at the right hand of God.

It manifests itself on earth as it is in Heaven. Stephen physically saw the glory of the Lord and Jesus himself said if we believe we will see the glory of God.

Romans 8:16-18(NIV) The Spirit himself testifies with our spirit that we are God's children. Now if we are children, then we are heirs—heirs of God and co-heirs with Christ, if indeed we share in his sufferings in order that we may also share in his glory. I consider that our present sufferings are not worth comparing with the glory that will be revealed in us.

Prayer

Glory Lord! I want more of Your Glory. I want to stand in the Holy of Holies and worship You! How can I even express how grateful I am that Your Son Jesus took my place of being crucified for my sins. You sacrificed Your only Son to save my wretched soul! I want to feel You and touch You and tell You how much I love You! I want to know every single thing about You, I want to serve You with my life. I want to be so close to You that I hear Your Voice. When You say turn here and turn there I want to hear it and walk in the path You have called me to walk. I want to shout and declare who You are and Your Greatness to every living soul on earth. I want everyone to have the relationship with You that I have with You.

Lord, You gave me life where there was only death. You gave me peace where there was only turmoil. You gave me mercy where there was only condemnation. You gave me forgiveness when I couldn't forgive myself. You gave me strength when I couldn't lift my head up. You gave me grace to take one step at a time and move forward. I feel the cloud of Your Glory! Glory Lord! I want more of Your Glory!

Reflection

How can I unclutter my life to concentrate on spending more time with the Lord?

Conclusion

Now Go Forth!

"But the one who stands firm to the end will be saved. And this gospel of the kingdom will be preached in the whole world as a testimony to all nations, and then the end will come". Matthew 24:13-15(NIV)

So what's it all about? Do we get healthy spiritually and emotionally just for selfish reasons? No, we must take our trials and learn from them. Nothing that has happened in your life will be wasted. God will use every trial to prepare you to minister to those in the same situation. How can you have credibility with those hurting if you don't know what they are going through? So praise the Lord for every wrong in your life and ask Him to use it for good. We need to praise the Lord for what He is about to do. Praise Him for your wilderness experience! Moses had to go through the wilderness to be able to lead the people out of the wilderness. Praise God for our wilderness training. We must allow the Lord to heal us so we can go out and help those that are hurting in the same way. We are called to a higher purpose and that purpose is to go out and preach the good news of the gospel to the whole world. How do we do that? We do it by reaching one person at a time.

Accepting God's grace is putting one foot in front of the other and moving forward, one step at a time and trusting God that He knows where you are going even if you can't see the road ahead. His ability is so far greater than our small little minds can conceive.

Galatians 3:23-29 (NIV) Before the coming of this faith, we were held in custody under the law, locked up until the faith that was to come would be revealed. So the law was our guardian until Christ came that we might be justified by faith. Now that this faith has come, we are no longer under a guardian. So in Christ Jesus you are all children of God through faith, for all of you who were baptized into Christ have clothed yourselves with Christ. There is neither Jew nor Gentile, neither slave nor free, nor is there male and female, for you are all one in Christ Jesus. If you belong to Christ, then you are Abraham's seed, and heirs according to the promise.

Galatians 5:5 (NIV) It is for freedom that Christ has set us free. Stand firm, then, and do not let yourselves be burdened again by a yoke of slavery.

Galatians 5:13 (NIV) You, my brothers and sisters, were called to be free. But do not use your freedom to indulge the flesh; rather, serve one another humbly in love. For the entire law is fulfilled in keeping this one command: "Love your neighbor as yourself." If you bite and devour each other, watch out or you will be destroyed by each other. So I say, walk by the Spirit, and you will not gratify the desires of the flesh. For the flesh desires what is contrary to the Spirit, and the Spirit what is contrary to the flesh. They are in conflict with each other, so that you are not to do whatever you want. But if you are led by the Spirit, you are not under the law.

So I challenge you to move forward, forgetting the past, using the wrongs that have led you to this very place in your life for good. Touch someone around you, you have been equipped with all the good things the Lord has for you in order to change lives. So many people around you are hurting so go forth and spread the good news of the gospel of Christ. We live because He loves us.

Drink from the living water that God has for you and you will never be thirsty again.

John 4: 9-15 (NIV)The Samaritan woman said to him, "You are a Jew and

I am a Samaritan woman. How can you ask me for a drink?" (For Jews do not associate with Samaritans. Jesus answered her, "If you knew the gift of God and who it is that asks you for a drink, you would have asked him and he would have given you living water."

"Sir," the woman said, "you have nothing to draw with and the well is deep. Where can you get this living water? Are you greater than our father Jacob, who gave us the well and drank from it himself, as did also his sons and his livestock?"

Jesus answered, "Everyone who drinks this water will be thirsty again, but whoever drinks the water I give them will never thirst. Indeed, the water I give them will become in them a spring of water welling up to eternal life." The woman said to him, "Sir, give me this water so that I won't get thirsty and have to keep coming here to draw water."

My prayer for you

Heavenly Father, creator of all things, open our eyes and ears to who we were created to be. Give us supernatural understanding of our worth in You. Help us to grasp and truly understand that we are heirs to the throne just like Your Son because of Your sacrifice of His life on the cross. We give praise and thanksgiving to our Lord Jesus for giving His life for ours and for taking the keys of Hell from the enemy so we can have everlasting life. We pray for complete healing of past hurts and for peace. We worship You and thank You for everything You are. In Jesus wonderful healing name. Amen

REFERENCES

http://en.wikipedia.org/wiki/Samaria_(ancient_city) 11-18-12

http://www.constitution.org/col/amazing_grace-p.html 11-17-12

http://www.biography.com/people/grace-kelly-9362226

http://www.helpguide.org/mental/domestic_violence_abuse_types_signs_causes_effects.htm retrieved 11-06-12

https://www.facebook.com/drmarkchironna?fref=ts retrieved 11-10-12

http://www.bibletribes.org/benjamin/introduction

http://www.truthaboutdeception.com/cheating-and-infidelity/stats-about-infidelity.html retrieved 11-20-12

Buss, D. M., & Shackelford, T. K. (1997).Susceptibility to infidelity in the first year of marriage. Journal of Research in Personality, 31, 193-221.

http://www.goodtherapy.org/blog/warning-signs-of-bad-therapy/ retrieved 11-23-12

http://www.merriam-webster.com/dictionary/praise retrieved 11-23-12

http://www.studylight.org/dic/hbd/view.cgi?number=T5086 retrieved 11-23-12

http://www.merriam-webster.com/dictionary/hallowed retrieved 11-23-12

http://lifestream.org/blog/2013/01/12/kintsukuro-how-broken-pottery-becomes-art/ retrieved 1-26-13

www.ingramcontent.com/pod-product-compliance
Ingram Content Group UK Ltd.
Pitfield, Milton Keynes, MK11 3LW, UK
UKHW041933190726
13854UKWH00004B/1563

9 781449 783310